TRAINS

Jean Coppendale

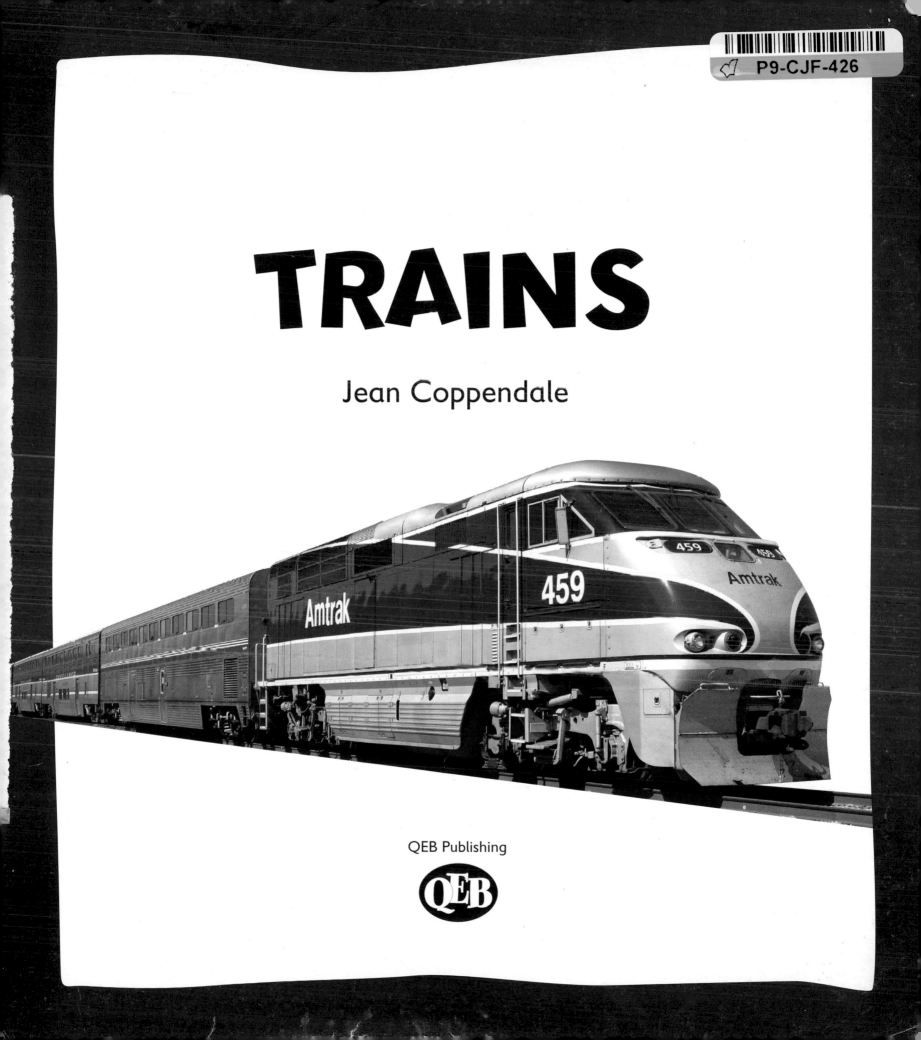

QEB Publishing

QEB

First published in the United States by
QEB Publishing, Inc.
23062 La Cadena Drive
Laguna Hills, CA 92653

www.qeb-publishing.com

Library of Congress Control Number: 2007000920

ISBN 978-1-59566-502-7

Written by Jean Coppendale
Designed by Chhaya Sajwan (Q2A Media)
Editor Katie Bainbridge
Picture Researcher Lalit Dalal (Q2A Media)

Publisher Steve Evans
Creative Director Zeta Davies
Senior Editor Hannah Ray

Printed and bound in China

Picture credits
Key: t = top, b = bottom, c = center,
l = left, r = right, FC = front cover
Joe Osciak: with thanks for image on page 4–5
SBB AG, Bern - Fotodienst/Alain D. Boillat: 5
Jtb Photo Communications Inc/Photolibrary: 6–7, 19
The Glacier Express: 7 t: **Louie Schoeman:** 8–9
CORBIS: Paul A. Souders 9 t
Dave Toussaint Photography: 10–11, 20–21
Paul Lantz: 11 b: **ALSTOM Transport:** 12–13
Denis Baldwin: 14–15
Alamy: Gunter Marx 16–17, Peter Titmuss 17 t
Photo by Fred Guenther: 18–19
Getty: Bruce Hands FC

Words in **bold** can be found
in the glossary on page 23.

Contents

What is a **train?**

Trains are used to carry people from one place to another. They also carry **goods**, such as cars and coal. A train moves along on tracks.

Some trains carry **passengers** from one city to another.

At the front of the train is the driver's cab. This is where the driver sits and makes the train start and stop.

Train travel

Trains can travel anywhere there is a track. They can climb mountains and speed across deserts. Trains travel over water using bridges and under water using **tunnels**.

Trains sometimes travel through beautiful countryside.

ROCKY MOUNTAINEER RAILTOURS

In Switzerland, trains travel through mountains covered in snow.

In some places, trains travel through tunnels that are cut into the mountains. They do this if the mountains are too high or too steep to climb.

Steam trains

The first trains used **steam** to make them move. Steam trains have huge **furnaces** with roaring fires inside. The fire heats water in order to make steam. The steam then powers the engine.

Some steam trains are still in use today. This steam train takes **tourists** along the coast of Namibia, in Africa.

3321

The furnace is at the front of the train. Workers shovel coal into the furnace throughout the journey to keep the train moving.

Keeping the fires burning is a dirty job. It's also a very hot job!

Freight trains

Freight or cargo trains are used to carry different loads from one place to another. It is cheap and fast to transport big, heavy loads by train.

A train with lots of wagons can carry huge loads across the country. The wagons can also make the train very long!

All sorts of goods, such as vegetables, furniture, and bricks, are carried by freight trains. Freight trains usually travel a long way.

This freight train is carrying new cars to the car dealer.

Everyday trains

Some trains take people to work in the morning and bring them home again in the evening. These are called **commuter trains**. Commuter trains can get crowded during **rush hour**. Sometimes there are not enough seats for everyone.

Many big cities have underground trains that take people to work and school.

89 S 1021

Skytrains

Some trains travel high above the ground. They are called skytrains. These trains move on tracks that are built like a bridge. Skytrains are useful in busy places where there are many people.

Many airports and **amusement parks** have skytrains. They can quickly move people a short distance.

This skytrain is in Detroit, Michigan. It does not have a driver because it is controlled by a computer.

This skytrain is called a Maglev. It does not have wheels. Instead, it moves using **magnets**.

Water—no problem!

Trains are heavy, so a bridge carrying a train has to be very strong.

Big bridges are built over lakes and rivers so that trains can travel across water. Some bridges have both a road and train tracks. Cars and trains can cross these bridges at the same time.

Some trains travel under the water. They go through special tunnels.

The Channel Tunnel is a long tunnel under the ocean. It connects England to France. Cars can drive onto a special train that takes them through the tunnel.

Express trains

Some trains quickly carry passengers long distances. These are called express trains. They stop at only a few stations and travel very fast.

This tilting train travels very fast.

Some express trains can **tilt** slightly as they go around **curves** in the track. This is so they do not have to slow down.

Some trains have huge windows and a glass roof. Passengers can enjoy the view as they travel!

Sleeper cars

Some passenger trains have to travel long distances through the night. These trains have special **cars** called sleeper cars. In sleeper cars, passengers can sleep and even take a shower in the morning!

These kinds of trains also have a restaurant on board where people can eat.

Some train trips last for many days, so it is important to have a comfortable bed.

Activities

- Collect train pictures from magazines. Put them in a book or on the wall in groups, such as: trains that carry people, steam trains, or trains crossing a bridge.

- Look at this train. Do you think this is a steam train? Why?

- Make up a story about a train. What kind of train is it? Where is it going? What is it carrying? What happens during the trip?

- Have you been on a train recently? Where were you going? Who were you with? Did you enjoy it? Was the train fast or slow? Full or empty? Draw a picture of yourself on the train.

- Look at these three pictures. Which one shows train tracks?

  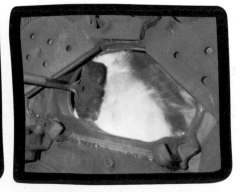

Glossary

Amusement parks
Parks with rides, games, and vendors.

Cargo
Items carried from one place to another by train. Also called freight.

Cars
The parts of a train where the passengers sit.

Commuter trains
Trains that take people to and from their place of work.

Curves
Lines that bend.

Freight
Items carried from one place to another by train. Also called cargo.

Furnaces
The places where fire burns to make steam for the train's engine.

Goods
Things that are bought and sold.

Loads
A large amount of something that is carried from one place to another.

Magnets
Magnets use an invisible force to pull metal things toward them or push metal things away from them. This force is called magnetism.

Passengers
People who pay to travel on trains.

Rush hour
Time of the day when large numbers of people travel to and from work.

Steam
Clouds of gas that come from boiling water.

Tilt
When something leans to one side.

Tourist
Someone who travels for pleasure.

Tunnels
Underground passageways for trains.

Index